20TH CENTURY SCIENCE & TECHNOLOGY

1940-60

THE NUCLEAR AGE

Steve Parker

Heinemann
LIBRARY

CONTENTS

The first space traveller was a dog, Laika. She was carried on board the Sputnik 2 satellite in 1957 and helped to pave the way for human beings in space.

Windscale reactor in north-west England was one of the first large-scale nuclear power stations opened in the 1950s. The site is now known as Sellafield.

20TH CENTURY SCIENCE & TECHNOLOGY

1 THE 0 AGE

PARKER, Steve

1940-60, the nuclear age

20TH CENTURY SCIENCE & TECHNOLOGY – 1940-60
was produced by

David West ⚇ Children's Books

7 Princeton Court
55 Felsham Road
London SW15 1AZ

Designers: Jenny Skelly & Aarti Parmar
Editor: James Pickering
Picture Research: Brooks Krikler Research

First published in Great Britain in 2000 by
Heinemann Library, Halley Court, Jordan Hill,
Oxford OX2 8EJ, a division of Reed Educational and
Professional Publishing Limited.

OXFORD MELBOURNE AUCKLAND
JOHANNESBURG BLANTYRE GABORONE
IBADAN PORTSMOUTH (NH) USA CHICAGO

Copyright © 2000 David West Children's Books

04 03 02 01 00
10 9 8 7 6 5 4 3 2 1

ISBN 0 431 12192 3 (HB)
ISBN 0 431 12199 0 (PB)

British Library Cataloguing in Publication Data

Parker, Steve, 1952 -
1940 - 1960 the nuclear age -
(Twentieth century science & technology).
1. Technology - History - 20th century -
Juvenile literature
2. Science - History - 20th century -
Juvenile literature
3. Aeronautics - Juvenile literature
I. Title
609' .044

Printed and bound in Italy

PHOTO CREDITS :
Abbreviations: t-top, m-middle, b-bottom,
r-right, l-left, c-centre.

Cover Hulton Getty Collection, Corbis.
Pages 4tl & b, 6t & bl, 8-9, 10, 11m, 12
all, 13b, 15l, 16-17, 17 all, 18, 19 both,
20 both, 21, 22t, 24b, 26 both, 26-27, 28
both, 28-29 & 29t - Hulton Getty
Collection. 6br, 7 both, 15r, 16t, 22b, 22-
23, 25 all, 29b - Corbis. 8 both, 9, 10-11,
11t, 13t, 24t & 27tl - AKG London. 14t -
Solution Pictures. 14b & 23 - David
West. 18-19 - Union Pacific Museum
Collection. 27tr - Corbis Images.

*The dates in brackets after a person's
name give the years that he or she lived.*

*An explanation of difficult words can be
found in the glossary on page 30.*

WAR AND PEACE

The 1940s began with the world at war. Military scientists had devised weapons of huge power that killed millions of people in Europe, North Africa and Asia.

But another scientific development helped to bring World War 2 to a swift end – the atomic bomb. As the conflict subsided, the awesome power of the atom was put to more peaceful uses in nuclear power stations. However the 1950s saw new tensions as two great superpowers arose. The USA and many countries of Western Europe grouped together, as did the USSR (former Soviet Union) and its neighbours in Eastern Europe. Their superpower rivalry speeded technological progress, not only in military areas such as nuclear missiles, but also in more peaceful areas such as jet travel, new materials, radio and television, and early electronic computers. The end of the 1950s saw another great rivalry based on scientific progress – the Space Race.

The 'Flying Bedstead' of 1955 was one of many strange vehicles made for aircraft research.

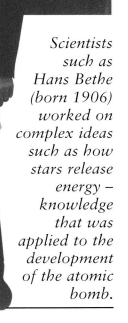

Scientists such as Hans Bethe (born 1906) worked on complex ideas such as how stars release energy – knowledge that was applied to the development of the atomic bomb.

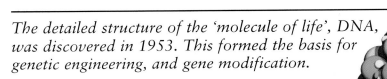

The detailed structure of the 'molecule of life', DNA, was discovered in 1953. This formed the basis for genetic engineering, and gene modification.

BIG IDEAS

Technology played a great part in World War 2 (1939-45). After the conflict many countries set up scientific research centres. Teams worked on practical projects such as faster planes and better radio, and also on academic questions such as how the Universe began and the secret of life itself.

By the 1950s science, once an obscure option in schools and colleges, was a major subject.

IN THE BEGINNING

The idea that the Universe began with a Big Bang had been suggested in the 1920s. During the 1940s, scientists carried out test nuclear explosions and also built larger, more powerful particle accelerators or 'atom-smasher' machines. Their studies showed how energy changed into atomic particles during the first seconds after the Big Bang.

James Watson (born 1928)

Hans Bethe (left) began a new branch of physics (below) while travelling home on a train after a meeting.

A VITAL THEORY

Quantum electrodynamics, QED, was developed from 1947. It explains how the particles called electrons orbit the nucleus (centre) of an atom. When electrons move from one orbit to another within an atom, they give off a precise amount of energy. The energy levels within an atom can be compared to a flight of stairs. The amount of energy is precise because the electron can only go down one 'step' at a time. QED is often called 'the most accurate theory in physics'.

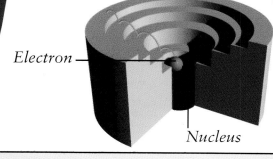

Electron

Nucleus

6

THE BLUEPRINT OF LIFE

Francis Crick (born 1916)

Since about 1900, biologists suspected that each living thing developed according to a plan or 'blueprint' of instructions inherited from its parents. The instructions, called genes, were in the form of a chemical substance. In 1944, US biologist Oswald Theodore Avery (1877–1955) showed that this substance was de-oxyribonucleic acid, DNA. Many researchers tried to discover the structure of DNA and how it could be copied to pass on genes. British biologist Francis Crick and US zoologist James Watson succeeded in 1953 at the Cavendish Laboratories in Cambridge, England. They found DNA was a double helix (left). Their discovery was hailed as one of the most important in the entire history of science.

DNA carries genetic instructions, in the form of a chemical code, for how a living thing grows and maintains itself. Crick and Watson found that DNA's shape was a double helix, like two ladders twisted around each other. The ladders or strands separate and each one makes a copy of its partner, so the genes can be passed on.

7

POWER IN THE ATOM

The smallest piece of chemical substance is an atom. In the 1910s Albert Einstein predicted that if atoms are split apart, tiny bits of them could change into gigantic amounts of energy. This was how the atomic bomb worked.

J Robert Oppenheimer (1904–67) discusses a scientific problem with Albert Einstein in 1951.

THE SCIENTIFIC WAR

More than any other conflict, World War 2 was decided by science and military technology. The ultimate weapon, the atomic bomb, was developed in the US from 1942 under the secret code name of the Manhattan Project. Physicist J Robert Oppenheimer led the research team at the Los Alamos Laboratories, New Mexico. Their first test explosion was on 16 July 1945.

A vast cloud rises above Hiroshima, Japan from the atomic bomb explosion of 1945. It devastated two-thirds of the city.

ATOMIC DEVASTATION

One month later two atomic bombs were dropped on to Japanese cities. Hiroshima suffered the first blast on 6 August, and Nagasaki was hit three days later. The result was more than 120,000 deaths, at least as many injuries, and horrifying destruction. The end of the war came soon after, on 2 September 1945.

Models of the atomic bombs: 'Little Boy' (front) fell on Hiroshima and 'Fat Man' (rear) on Nagasaki.

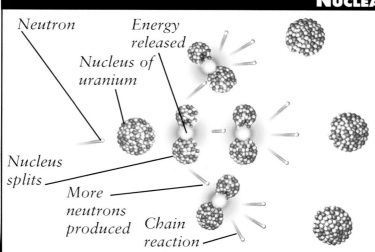

Neutron

Energy released

Nucleus of uranium

Nucleus splits

More neutrons produced

Chain reaction

The atomic bomb obtained its power from the splitting, or fission, of the nuclei (centres) of atoms. The Hiroshima bomb used the substance uranium-235 as its raw material. Inside the bomb two fist-sized lumps smashed together in a device like a gun barrel. The shock caused a few nuclei of uranium to split, giving off energy as heat and radiation, and also releasing extra particles called neutrons. These hit more uranium nuclei, causing them to split, and so on in a chain reaction. In less than a second this produced the massive explosion. The Nagasaki bomb was similar, but its raw material was plutonium-239.

HARMFUL TO USEFUL

After the war, arguments about the use of such awesome weapons raged to and fro. Some of the project scientists were so distraught by the terrible results that they committed suicide. Others said that the atomic bombs hastened the end of the war and so saved further fighting and bloodshed. Should atomic research continue? Many people agreed that the scientists themselves were not to blame and scientific progress could not stand still. But the results should be used to benefit rather than destroy humankind. One line of research led to nuclear power stations (see page 20).

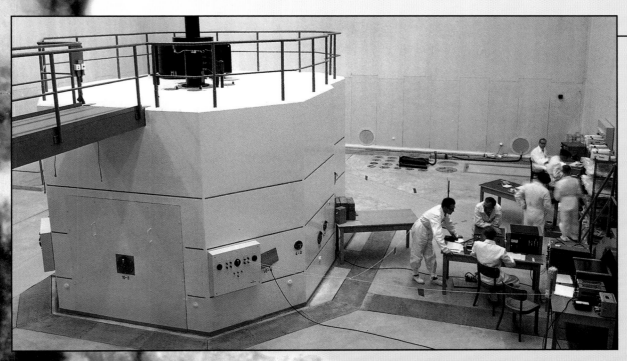

An atomic bomb uses an uncontrolled chain reaction. Moderator substances absorb some of the energy and particles and control the process. The first controlled chain reaction was at the University of Chicago, USA in 1942. In the 1950s many research centres built test reactors, like this one at Germany's Hahn-Meitner Institute.

FASTER AND HIGHER

During the 1930s, aero-engineers had tested a new form of aircraft engine, the jet. During the 1940s, jets improved dramatically in power and became much more reliable and efficient. They were fitted to fighter and bomber planes, as military aircraft from different air forces tried to outdo each other by flying faster, higher and farther.

THE JET AGE

British engineer Frank Whittle (1907–96) developed jet engines at Farnborough, England during the 1930s. The first jet aircraft to fly was the Heinkel He178 in 1939, designed by German engineer Ernst Heinkel. It was mainly a test craft not intended for mass production but it showed the potential of jet power. Various air forces worked to develop jet planes during World War 2, the most successful being the Messerschmitt Me262. But it did not come into service until near the end of 1944, too late to affect the conflict. After the war jet engines soon took over from propellers in military planes, as the USA and USSR superpowers built up air power (see page 17).

Ernst Heinkel (1888–1958) studies designs for one of the German Heinkel propeller aircraft, in 1941. His He178 jet (above right) first flew in August 1939.

The first British jet plane to fly was the Gloster E28/39 in May 1941, powered by a Whittle engine. The Gloster Meteor fighter of 1944 was developed from it.

FIRST HELI-RESCUE

Like the jet, the helicopter was developed during the 1930s. But the war effort concentrated on normal fixed-wing aircraft rather than rotary-winged helicopters (see below). Nevertheless in 1943 Sikorsky R-4 helicopters went into service with the US Air Force. In April 1944 one R-4 hoisted four stranded air crew to safety in the Pacific campaign of World War 2. This was the first ever helicopter rescue.

HELICOPTERS GROW UP

Military chiefs quickly saw the rescue potential of the helicopter and soon many air forces had them. During the Korean War (1950–53) bubble-canopied Bell 47 helicopters airlifted more than 20,000 wounded soldiers to safety in MASH (Mobile Army Surgical Hospital) units. The search and rescue powers of the helicopter were also taken up by police, coastguards and highway patrols. The 'chopper' had become vital for emergency and rescue services.

The first large helicopter was the US PV-3, shown here undergoing trials in 1945.

HOW THE HELICOPTER WORKS

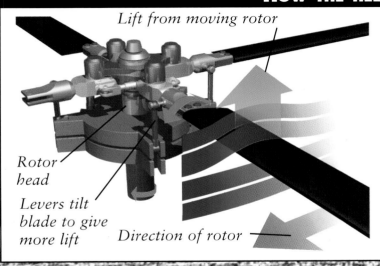

Lift from moving rotor

Rotor head

Levers tilt blade to give more lift

Direction of rotor

An ordinary plane wing has a curved upper surface and a flatter lower surface, known as the aerofoil shape. As the wing moves through the air, this shape creates a lifting force that makes the plane rise. The rotor blade of a helicopter is like a very long, narrow wing. It has the same aerofoil shape. As it spins or rotates it creates lift in the same way. But the rotor can spin and generate lift even when the helicopter itself is not moving. This is how helicopters hover in mid air, and it is also why they are called rotary-wing aircraft. A complex set of levers in the rotor head (see left) tilt the rotor blades so the helicopter can turn, climb, dive and even fly backwards.

RACE INTO SPACE

As the superpowers of the USSR and USA built up their armed forces, they also wanted to impress the world with their scientific achievements. Two great challenges of the age were to fly faster than sound, and to fly away from Earth altogether – into space.

'COLD WAR' SCIENCE

These challenges were not only good publicity. The fastest planes would have an advantage in war, and space could be used for spy satellites and even orbiting weapons. Also the 1950s was the time of the 'Cold War'. There was no actual fighting between the two great powers but tensions were very high.

THE SOUND BARRIER

The speed of sound is about 1,060 kilometres per hour at great height. Some aircraft shook badly as they neared this speed and the idea grew that there was a 'sound barrier'. Would breaking it be like flying into a brick wall? On 14 October 1947 US test pilot Charles Yeager finally flew faster than sound without harm, in his Bell X-1 rocket plane.

Captain Charles 'Chuck' Yeager, on the left in the photo above, called his X-1 plane Glamorous Glennis *after his wife. On the right he is at the controls.*

Photograph of Laika who was blasted into orbit in Sputnik 2. At the time it was said she parachuted back to Earth. In fact she died in space.

FIRST INTO SPACE

During the mid 1950s both the USA and USSR secretly worked on rockets powerful enough to lift a craft into space, in orbit around the Earth. It was widely believed that the USA had more advanced technology and would be first. On 4 October 1957 came news that the USSR had launched the world's first space craft, the ball-shaped satellite Sputnik 1. It was quickly followed on 3 November by Sputnik 2 carrying the first living thing into space – a mongrel dog, Laika.

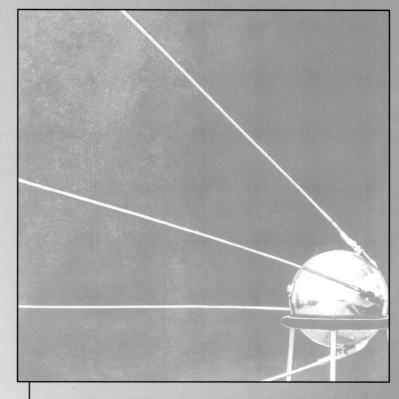

Sputnik 1 was an aluminium ball 58 cm across containing a radio transmitter and thermometer.

Before the launch of Sputnik 2, the Soviets sent dog-carrying rockets 100 kilometres into the upper atmosphere.

THE FIRST SPACE TRAVELLERS

The name *Sputnik* means 'travelling companion' in the Russian language. Sputnik 1 weighed just 84 kg and Sputnik 2 some 510 kg. A rocket must reach a speed called escape velocity, 11.2 km/sec, in order to get free of the pull of Earth's gravity and enter space. The USA's first satellite was Explorer 1, launched on 31 January 1958.

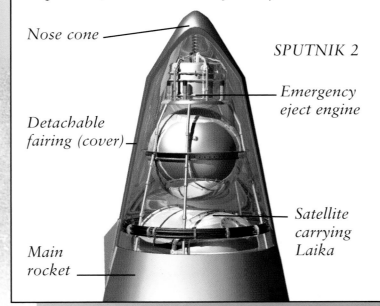

Nose cone

SPUTNIK 2

Emergency eject engine

Detachable fairing (cover)

Satellite carrying Laika

Main rocket

CONNECTIONS

In the 1950s, exchange of scientific information speeded up. There were many new technical journals, telephones and radios in most homes, and television was spreading fast. 'Spin-offs' began to appear, where an invention or development in one area of science was adapted for others.

CODE-CRACKERS TO COMPUTERS

War is a time for secrecy when armed forces send messages in code. Various methods for coding by mechanical machines were developed during World War 2. After the war some of these were adapted for the first electronic computers (see page 7). In 1951 Remington Rand's Univac 1 became the first commercially available large computer, storing information on reels of magnetic tape.

German forces used Enigma code machines in World War 2. But a specialized 'dedicated' computer, Colossus, helped to break them.

MESSAGES BY LIGHT

Optical fibres (fibre-optics) are thin, flexible rods of special glass or plastic, narrower than hairs. Messages pass along them as a code of light flashes. The light beam reflects off the fibre's inner surface, zig-zagging even round curves. The first optical fibres were produced in London, England in 1955. However it was the development of the laser during the 1960s which made the light pulses powerful enough for practical use.

Fibre-optic lamp

Light beam internally reflected

Fibre (rod of glass)

14

THE UNDERWATER WORLD

Submarines played an important part in World War 2. But at first, naval divers were limited to a heavy suit with an air tube to the surface. In 1943 a team led by French navy officer Jacques Cousteau developed SCUBA, Self-Contained Underwater Breathing Apparatus, also called the aqualung. This was soon being used by navy divers or 'frogmen' and after the war by underwater explorers, photographers, archaeologists, oceanographers and other scientists.

From the 1950s Jacques Cousteau (1910–97) became a famous marine film-maker and conservationist.

Scuba divers wear a tank on the back, which contains air or a special mixture of gases for breathing. The very high pressure of the air is reduced by a regulator. As divers breathe in, a flexible flap or diaphragm works a valve that allows air into the mouth. Breathing out closes this valve and opens another so the stale air can be released into the water.

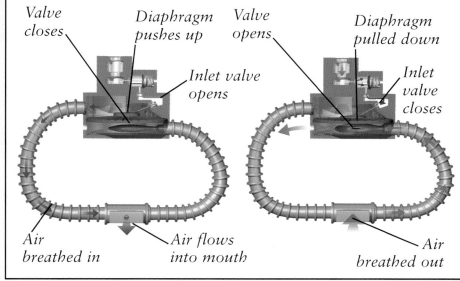

Valve closes
Diaphragm pushes up
Inlet valve opens
Air breathed in
Air flows into mouth

Valve opens
Diaphragm pulled down
Inlet valve closes
Air breathed out

TV DINNERS

Freezing to preserve foods had been developed in the 1910s. During the 1930s, the techniques of freeze-drying, developed for medical products, were adapted for the food industry. By the 1940s whole pre-cooked meals could be bought frozen, stored in the deep-freezer and then heated when required. The great convenience of these ready-made meals, along with the spread of television, led to the 1950s idea of the 'TV dinner'.

Convenience foods became very popular in the 1950s, especially in the USA. The foods were preserved by freezing, as shown here, or by canning or bottling.

15

ON THE MOVE

The 1950s marked the start of the 'Jet Age'. Long-distance travel suddenly became much faster with the introduction of 'jetliners'. These large, passenger-carrying aircraft were powered by jet engines developed from military fighter and bomber planes. They whisked people around the world twice as fast as propeller aircraft and twenty times more quickly than ocean liners.

The Boeing 707 first flew in July 1954 and was in large-scale production by 1957. It was larger and faster than the Comet, cruising at 880 km/h.

DISASTER

The first jetliner in regular service was the British de Havilland Comet in 1952. It was closely followed by the American Boeing 707. But 1954 saw two Comet crashes, both in Italy. All Comets were grounded. Painstaking work on the wrecks showed that the problem was metal fatigue (weakening and cracking). In the meantime, the Boeing went on to become a world best-seller.

The early Comets carried about 40 passengers at 780 km/h, far faster than any propeller plane.

HOW A JET ENGINE WORKS

A jet has two sets of angled blades called turbines that spin on a central shaft. The front set suck in air and squeeze or compress it. Jet fuel sprays into the air and is ignited in a continuous roaring explosion. The gases blast past a rear set of turbines that spin and power the front ones. The gases then roar out of the back and their rearward thrust pushes the engine forwards.

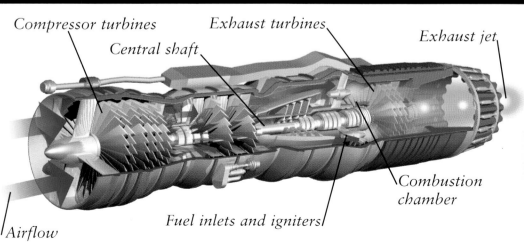

Compressor turbines

Exhaust turbines

Central shaft

Exhaust jet

Combustion chamber

Fuel inlets and igniters

Airflow

ON HOLIDAY

Jetliners could fly higher than propeller planes and so avoid bad weather at low altitudes. This made journeys safer and more reliable. The arrival of fast, long-distance travel saw a revolution in tourism, particularly the rise of the package holiday. People could fly to an exotic holiday destination in a few hours. By the late 1950s in developed nations, about one holiday in ten was a 'package'.

Rolls Royce 'Flying Bedstead' test craft

BEST OF BOTH

As jet fighters and helicopters improved, aero engineers wondered if the speed of the first could be combined with the hovering ability of the second. The 'Flying Bedstead' of 1955 directed the blast from its jet engines straight down so it could hover. It eventually led to the Harrier 'jump jet' of the 1970s.

COLD WAR IN THE SKIES

As the 1950s continued, the superpowers of the USSR and USA both tried to build faster, more agile, longer-range aircraft. The main advances were in new alloys (combinations of metals) to withstand the enormous stresses and temperatures inside jet engines, and also the heat generated on the craft's outer 'skin' by flying so fast through the air.

The first jet air combat took place in 1950, during the Korean war. A Soviet built Mig was downed by an American Sabre. Pictured are the Mig 17 (right) and the F–86 Sabre (far right).

SHIPS AND TRAINS

The Jet Age of high-speed air travel began in the 1950s. It was fast and convenient – but very expensive. Most people still went on long journeys overland by rail and across the sea by ship. However cars and trucks were becoming more common too. As all these modes of transport began to compete with each other, some had to lose out.

POST-WAR REVIVAL

The railways had suffered from the worldwide economic depression of the 1930s, especially in the USA and other rich nations. However they went through a revival during World War 2 when they were used to transport heavy military materials and hardware. In the early 1950s, diesel and diesel-electric locomotives began to replace the noisier, dirtier and less efficient steam engines. Even so the convenience of cars and the speed of planes began to take over. By the end of the 1950s, the railways were beginning to suffer from lack of business.

Union Pacific's largest steam locomotive, 'Big Boy', was replaced in 1959 by diesel-electric power.

18

> ### ⬤ ROUND THE WORLD UNDERWATER ⬤
> The US Navy's *Nautilus* was launched in 1954. It was 98 metres long, had a crew of 105 and cruised at 37 km/h. One advantage of its nuclear (atomic) power plant was that, unlike most types of engines, it did not burn fuel and so needed no air. This meant *Nautilus* could circle the world without surfacing. In 1958, it travelled to the North Pole and across the Arctic Ocean – all under the polar ice cap.
>
> *Nautilus on sea trials in 1955*
>
>

NUCLEAR CRAFT

Would the science of nuclear power spread from missiles and electricity generation into transport? A nuclear reactor was far too heavy for a plane, but it could be fitted into a ship. The first nuclear-powered craft was the USA's submarine *Nautilus* in 1954, followed by the USSR's icebreaker *Lenin* in 1959.

The United States Lines' United States covered 5,465 kilometres at an average of 66 km/h on its first voyage in 1952.

WATER CRAFT

To attract both passengers and publicity, the 'Blue Riband' was awarded for the fastest crossing of the Atlantic by ship or boat. In July 1952 the USA's *United States* ocean liner, powered by a new design of steam turbine, smashed the record by more than 10 hours. Journey time between New York and London or Paris was reduced to four days. But jetliners could do the trip in six hours. Ocean liners could not compete for speed so they offered great luxury instead.

A NEW TYPE OF CRAFT

In 1954 British inventor Christopher Cockerell had the idea for a craft that would float on a cushion of air. It could ride above the waves and also float over smooth land. His first hovercraft, SR N-1, flew in 1959. The lifting force came from a large down-pointing fan.

Downward fan (lifter)

Forward fan (propeller)

Hovercraft at rest

Air trapped by flexible skirt

Christopher Cockerell (1910–99) and his wife prepare to board an early hovercraft service.

ON THE MAKE

One of the most far-reaching inventions in the history of science is the nuclear (atomic) weapon (see page 8). It has the ability to destroy the world with both its explosive power and its radioactive pollution. However nuclear power has had peaceful uses too, especially in electricity generation and on a much smaller scale in medicine.

CONTROL ROD MECHANISM

THE GREAT NEW HOPE

In the 21st century we are aware of the many problems posed by electricity-generating nuclear power stations, including the possibility of terrible accidents and the rising piles of radioactive waste. But back in the 1950s nuclear power was seen as a great hope for solving the world's energy crisis. When oil, coal, gas and other fossil fuels for power stations eventually ran out, nuclear power would be the safe, clean alternative for the future. Many countries began to build large nuclear power stations.

An early safety precaution was to site nuclear power stations away from cities. Windscale (see page 4) was in rural north-west England.

Fuel rod

Control rod

Moderator matrix

In a nuclear power station, a chain reaction occurs as nuclei of uranium fuel split in nuclear fission. They release heat and atomic particles called neutrons (shown as purple lines above, see also page 9). To stop the reaction getting out of control, a moderator substance slows down the neutrons and control rods (usually made of boron) absorb excess ones.

In 1956 Calder Hall, in north-west England, became the world's first large-scale nuclear power plant to generate electricity. This view shows control rods being adjusted inside the reactor below.

A CND rally at Aldermaston, England

BAN THE BOMB! People in the 1950s gradually became aware of the terrifying prospect of a nuclear war. In 1958 the Campaign for Nuclear Disarmament, CND, began. Protesters went on marches and held demonstrations, to persuade countries with nuclear weapons to get rid of them.

THE NUCLEAR POWER STATION

The power station is dominated by a huge dome of steel and concrete, the containment vessel. It is designed to stop heat and radiation escaping in an accident. Inside is the nuclear reactor which generates heat in its core, to boil circulating water into steam in the primary circuit. Heat is transferred through an exchanger to a secondary circuit, where the water is separate from the reactor core for safety reasons. The heat in the secondary circuit is used to spin huge turbine blades which are attached to electricity generators as in other types of power station.

Reactor vessel

Superheated steam

Heat exchanger

To turbines

From turbines

Reactor core

Primary circuit

Cooled water returns

Secondary circuit

Containment vessel

Reactor

Radiation shielding

Electricity transformers

Turbines and generators

Radioactive fuel and waste building

ARTIFICIAL AGE

In the 1920s-30s, research chemists had begun to produce artificial (laboratory-made) substances such as rayon, nylon and plastics. From the 1940s these substances started to replace more natural materials such as wood and leather in industry and daily life.

Huge factories were set up to spin artificial fibres such as nylon and weave cloth and garments from them. This nylon factory opened in Pontypool, Wales in 1953.

22

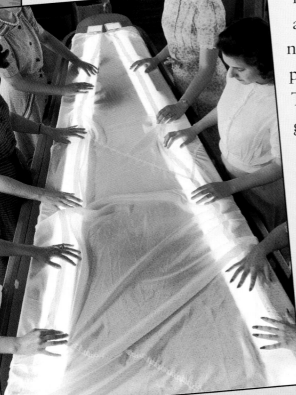

NYLON FOR EVERYONE

The new fibres such as nylon were light, strong and hard-wearing. They could be made in many thread thicknesses and bright colours. They did not rot or suffer attack by pests such as clothes moths. They also made smooth, sleek garments, especially sheer stockings. The first batch of stockings went on sale in the USA in 1940 and sold out within days. They soon replaced rayon stockings and became known simply as 'nylons'.

Natural fibres such as silk were still preferred for certain items like parachutes.

MAKING NYLON

The first types of nylon were made by heating together two chemicals, adipic acid and hexa-methylene-diamine, at 270°C. The resulting liquid cooled and was made into chips. These were then loaded into the spinning machine. Instead of twisting many short threads to make a yarn, as with natural fibres, this machine squirted hot, runny nylon out of small holes in a spinneret. The result was long, continuous filaments of nylon.

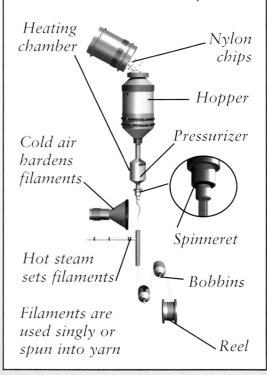

Heating chamber

Nylon chips

Hopper

Pressurizer

Cold air hardens filaments

Spinneret

Hot steam sets filaments

Bobbins

Filaments are used singly or spun into yarn

Reel

Nylon stockings were put on to leg-shaped metal formers, then softened with steam heat so they 'set' to the shape of the formers.

PLASTIC PLUSES

The new plastics also had advantages over more traditional materials. Again they were light, strong, hard-wearing and long-lasting. They could be brightly coloured, moulded into smooth or intricate shapes with little waste, and mass-produced for cheapness. They were also good insulators and did not carry electricity, which was important as electrical gadgets became more common.

A strong, flexible plastic developed for gas masks in World War 2 was adapted in 1946 for odourless, non-toxic food containers. This was Tupperware.

NEW METHODS

The new generation of plastics required new methods of manufacturing them. Many were thermoplastics, becoming soft and even runny at high temperatures. This feature was used in the process of injection moulding where hot, soft, runny plastic was forced into a shaped mould. It cooled and hardened into the finished item which was released by opening the mould. This led to an explosion in mass-produced plastic items, especially toys. Unlike older die-cast metal toys, the new plastic ones had no sharp edges and no small screws to come loose and swallow!

INJECTION MOULDING

In the screw type of injection moulder, plastic pellets from a hopper enter a screw mechanism and are forced along past electric heating elements. These make the pellets hot, soft and runny or molten. The molten plastic squirts out of the end and is forced or injected at high pressure into the shaped space inside a mould. It takes on the shape of the mould and goes hard as it cools.

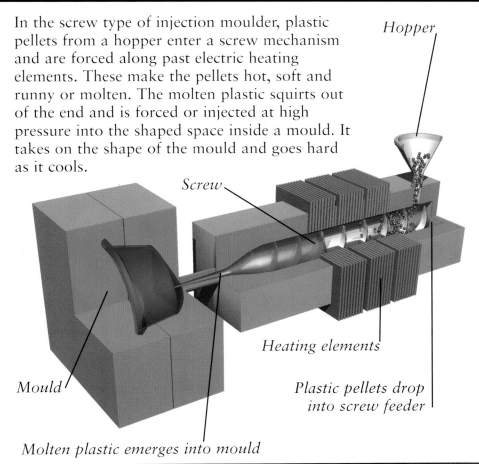

Hopper

Screw

Heating elements

Plastic pellets drop into screw feeder

Mould

Molten plastic emerges into mould

ELEC-TECH

The chaos and destruction of World War 2, especially in Europe, meant much rebuilding afterwards. Towns and cities grew again fully equipped with electrical power and telephone networks. Electric gadgets were central to everyday life.

Cinema enjoyed its greatest popularity during the 1950s. In the craze for '3-D' movies, the audience wore special spectacles which gave depth to the view on the flat screen.

SMALLER BUT BETTER

An enormous leap occurred in electrical technology in 1948. Many scientists were working with semiconductors such as germanium – materials that carry electricity only under certain conditions. Working at Bell Laboratories in the USA, one group discovered by accident a semiconductor device which could do the same jobs as the much larger valve or vacuum tube. The group included William Shockley (1910–89), John Bardeen (1908–91) and William Brattain (1902–87). They called their device a transistor.

Radios of the early 1940s were large, heavy pieces of furniture. By the late 1950s, transistor radios could easily be held in the hand (see page 29).

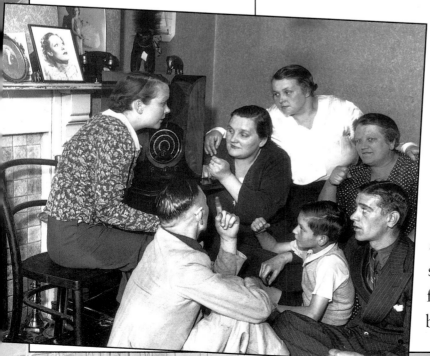

TRANSISTORS EVERYWHERE

Transistors revolutionized electronics. Compared with valves they were far smaller and lighter, used much less electricity, performed more reliably and coped with extreme conditions such as excess heat, cold and humidity. They also cost far less to manufacture. Transistors allowed many common electrical gadgets, such as radio sets, to be made only one-fifth of their former size and weight. They became truly portable (see page 29).

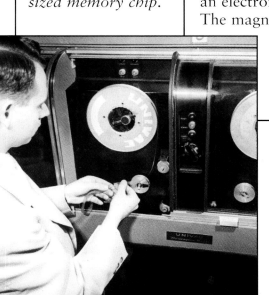

An operator loads a magnetic tape reel on to a 1954 computer. The bulky reel held one million times less information than a modern sugar-cube-sized memory chip.

Magnetic tape has a very thin coating of magnetic particles such as ferric (iron) oxide arranged at random. Electrical signals pass through a wire coil in the read-write head and turn it into an electromagnet of varying power. The magnetism makes the tape particles line up as the tape moves past, to record the information as micro-patches of magnetic code.

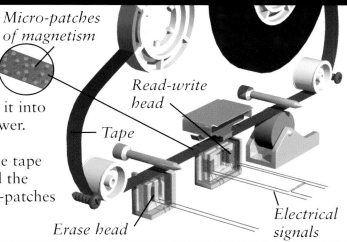

Micro-patches of magnetism

Read-write head

Tape

Erase head

Electrical signals

LIVE AND ON TAPE

The first tape recorders for storing information (data), as tiny patches of magnetism on a flexible tape, came into use in the late 1930s. At first they were used for sounds and music. During the 1950s, their use spread to the newly appearing computers and also into television. TV programmes no longer had to be sent out 'live'. They could be recorded on tape, edited and improved before they were broadcast. In the USA the year 1950 also saw the first experimental TV broadcasts in colour rather than black-and-white.

25

COLOUR ON THE SMALL SCREEN

Television spread rapidly during the 1950s but these were mainly black-and-white or monochrome sets. By 1958 there were some 50 million TV sets in the USA alone. Great historical events, such as the crowning of Queen Elizabeth II in 1953, caused a boost in sales. Several TV stations broadcast programmes in colour from about 1954. However by today's standards the pictures were small, blurred and had very bright, garish hues!

Watching a colour television set, 1954

A colour television camera, 1954

MEDICAL SCIENCE

Much medical progress during the 1940s-50s was due to advances in technology. Stronger, longer-lasting metal alloys and plastics led to improved artificial joints and other parts. The invention of the transistor made the life-saving device called the heart pacemaker so small that it could be implanted – put into the body.

A STEADY BEAT

Heart pacemakers are used for conditions called cardiac arrhythmias. The heart beats too fast or slow, or in an irregular way, or even stops. The pacemaker generates regular tiny electrical signals which are carried by wires into the heart muscle, stimulating it to contract and cause a heartbeat. The first operations to implant pacemakers into patients were in 1956.

Early heart pacemakers, like this 1958 model, were bulky and generated regular signals. Modern types vary the rate and strength of the signal according to the body's needs.

THE FIRST MAN

TO BECOME A WOMAN

In 1970 a movie was released telling the life story of American George/Christine Jorgensen. Here she poses beside a poster for the film.

MAN TO WOMAN

The 1950s were a time of more liberal ideas in society, including towards sex. In 1952, George Jorgensen became Christine Jorgensen in the first sex change operation – not a technically difficult process, but formerly frowned upon.

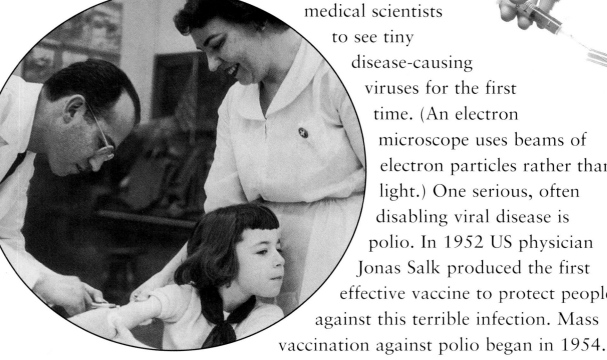

Jonas Salk (1914-95) vaccinates a young patient in 1954.

BETTER PROTECTION

In 1942, the electron microscope allowed medical scientists to see tiny disease-causing viruses for the first time. (An electron microscope uses beams of electron particles rather than light.) One serious, often disabling viral disease is polio. In 1952 US physician Jonas Salk produced the first effective vaccine to protect people against this terrible infection. Mass vaccination against polio began in 1954.

Salk's vaccine against poliomyelitis (polio) was given by injection. The modern version is taken by mouth, usually on a lump of sugar.

This 'artificial kidney' or renal dialysis machine dates from the early 1960s.

MORE ARTIFICIAL AIDS

Another life-saving device, the kidney dialysis machine, was tested in 1943. In some conditions the kidneys cannot do their normal task of cleaning and filtering the blood. So blood is led from the patient's body along a tube to the dialysis machine, which filters and purifies it before returning the blood to the patient. The patient is 'hooked up' to the machine for several hours, two or three times weekly.

SEEING INTO THE BODY

The most common way of seeing inside the body without cutting it open was the X-ray. But in the 1950s the dangers of X-rays were becoming clear. Another method introduced in 1958 is ultrasound. Very high-pitched or ultrasonic sound waves are beamed into the body. They reflect in different ways from various body tissues. The returning echoes are picked up by a microphone, analyzed by computer and shown as a picture.

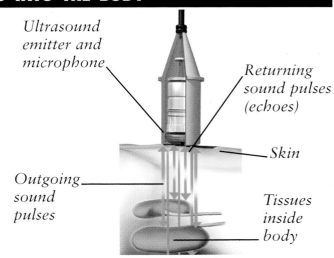

Ultrasound emitter and microphone

Returning sound pulses (echoes)

Skin

Outgoing sound pulses

Tissues inside body

GADGETS

By 1940 most domestic gadgets and appliances we know today, such as the vacuum cleaner and television, had been invented. The 1940s-50s saw improvements in their design and also a reduction in costs so that more people could buy them.

HI-TECH

The 1950s saw huge rises in consumer spending. People were leaving behind the hardship of the war years. Their earnings rose and inventions such as the transistor drove down prices. Former luxuries such as cars and televisions became necessities. For a much larger sum, about one year's wages, you could buy a computer with the first programme to give a human a reasonable game of chess – MANIC 1, developed in 1956.

The 'instant camera' produced photographs in a minute or two. Early versions were made from 1947 by Land. They are now known by the general name of 'polaroids'.

LOW-TECH

Among the less technical but extremely successful inventions of the time was the zipless fastener Velcro. Swiss engineer George de Mestral got the idea in 1948 after a walk in the woods, when spiky-hooked 'burr' seeds stuck to his socks and dog's fur. He patented his invention in 1955.

Aerosols or spray cans had been tested in 1926 but the technology to mass-produce them was not available until the 1940s.

MICROWAVE MAGIC

Microwaves are the same type of energy as radio and light, called electromagnetic energy. They are about 1 to 100 cm long and produced by a magnetron, in which an electric current changes direction or oscillates millions of times each second. The invisible waves make water molecules vibrate, spin and warm up, to heat and cook from within.

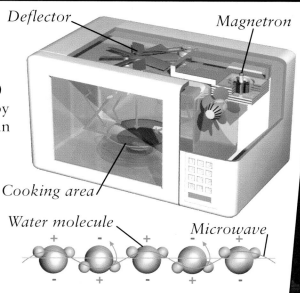

Deflector

Magnetron

Cooking area

Water molecule

Microwave

+ − + − +

− + − + −

An early domestic microwave oven dating from about 1947

Workers at a vinyl record factory listen to master discs in 1960 to check for flaws. The vinyl copies for sale are made by pressing from moulds of the metal master discs.

HI-FI AT HOME

1950 is regarded as the year when the 'hi-fi' became popular in the ordinary homes of industrial nations. 'Hi-fi' means high fidelity and refers to a good quality of sound reproduction. During the 1950s, vinyl records (first produced in 1948 by Columbia Records) and reel-to-reel tapes were sold in increasing numbers.

The Regency 'Pocket Radio' of 1954 needed a large pocket.

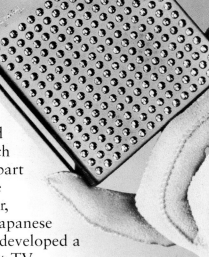

LESS MEANS MORE

The invention of the transistor (see page 24) affected all kinds of electrical equipment, from industrial machinery to consumer goods like the 'transistor' radio. The first commercial product to feature tiny, light transistors instead of hot, bulky valves was a hearing aid in 1952. Since transistors used much less electricity than valves, a great part of the reduction in size for portable equipment was the need for fewer, smaller batteries. By 1959, the Japanese company Sony had developed a transistorized pocket TV.

Valve

Transistor

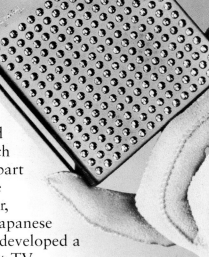

29

GLOSSARY

ALLOY A combination or 'mixture' of a metal with other substances, including other metals or non-metals. For example brass is an alloy of copper and zinc. Steel is an alloy of iron and carbon.

ATOM The smallest part of a pure substance (chemical element) that can exist naturally. Most atoms are made of three types of even tinier particles called protons, neutrons and electrons.

BIG BANG An event when everything began, including matter, such as atoms, space and also time.

DNA De-oxyribonucleic acid, the chemical substance which contains, in the form of a code, the instructions or genes for living things to grow and survive. Its double helix structure was discovered in 1953 by Watson and Crick (see pages 6-7)

FIXED-WING AIRCRAFT A normal type of aircraft where the wings stay still (see Rotary-wing aircraft).

MASS PRODUCTION The manufacture of standardized products in large quantities, usually by machines.

METAL FATIGUE When metal parts become weakened, bent, cracked and eventually snap or fail, due to repeated strain.

NUCLEAR FISSION When parts of the nucleus of an atom split apart, releasing vast amounts of energy.

NUCLEAR FUSION When parts of the nucleus of an atom join together, releasing vast amounts of energy.

OPTICAL FIBRE A hair-thin, flexible rod of transparent glass or plastic designed to carry information as coded flashes of light.

ROTARY-WING AIRCRAFT A type of aircraft where the wings spin around to create a lifting force, as in a helicopter (see Fixed-wing aircraft).

SATELLITE An object that goes round and round, or orbits, another object. The Moon is a natural satellite of the Earth. The term is generally used for artificial or man-made satellites launched by rockets.

'SPIN-OFF' An invention or development in one area of science or technology, which becomes adapted for another, originally unintended use.

30

WORLD EVENTS

- *Battle of Britain in World War Two* 19
- *USA enters War after attack on Pearl Harbour* 19
- *War rages in Pacific, Battle of Midway* 19
- *German forces surrender at Stalingrad* 19
- *Allied D-Day landings in Normandy, France* 19
- *Atom bombs dropped, World War Two ends* 19
- *First meetings of United Nations* 19
- *Indian region split into India and Pakistan* 19
- *Berlin Airlift as Russia blockades west of city* 19
- *China is Communist People's Republic* 19
- *Dalai Lama takes power in Tibet* 19
- *Libya becomes an independent country* 19
- *Elizabeth II comes to the throne in UK* 19
- *Failed revolution in Bolivia* 19
- *Communist Party banned in USA* 19
- *Strikes and revolution in Argentina* 19
- *Suez Canal crisis in Egypt* 19
- *Treaty of Rome begins 'Common Market'* 19
- *Iraq becomes a republic after coup* 19
- *Fidel Castro takes power in Cuba* 19

TIMELINE

	SCIENCE EVENTS	TECHNOLOGY	FAMOUS SCIENTISTS	INVENTIONS
40	•Prehistoric Lascaux cave paintings found	•First colour television broadcasts, USA	•Florey and Chain develop penicillin for patient use	•Nylon stockings go onto the mass market
41	•US President Roosevelt approves atom bomb work	•'Bug bomb' aerosol spray for insect pests	•Glenn Seaborg creates a form of element plutonium	•Terylene (dacron)
42	•Penicillin antibiotic in mass production	•Viruses seen at last, by electron microscopes	•Fermi's controlled nuclear chain reaction, Chicago	•Soft toilet paper (UK) •FIDO airport fog-clearer
43	•Colossus wartime code-cracking computer	•First artificial kidney machines	•Selman Waksman finds new antibiotic streptomycin	•SCUBA or aqualung
44	•V1 and V2 flying bomb missiles over England	•IBM Mark 1 'Controlled Calculator' computer	•Otto Hahn wins Nobel prize for atomic fission	•Plastic false eye
45	•Hiroshima and Nagasaki destroyed	•Eckert and Mauchly begin ENIAC computer	•Arthur C Clarke suggests idea of comms satellites	•Microwave oven patented
46	•First working nuclear reactor in USSR	•ENIAC, 18,000 valves and 30 tonnes, turned on	•Martin Ryle identifies first radio galaxy, Cygnus A	•Tupperware food and drink containers
47	•Theory of quantum electrodynamics devised	•First faster-than-sound flight, Yeager in Bell X-1	•Karl von Frisch discovers bees can see polarized light	•Tubeless tyres for automobiles
48	•Big Bang theory updated	•Shockley and colleagues invent the transistor	•Edwin Land devises 'instant' photographs	•Zipless fastener Velcro •Long-playing vinyl record
49	•First atomic test explosions in USSR	•First multistage rocket, a modified wartime V2	•Hebb suggests neural network memory in the brain	•Ready-prepared cake mixes go on sale
50	•First computer-aided weather forecasts	•Commercial colour TV introduces the 'advert'	•Jan Oort proposes the stellar cloud named after him	•Diner's Club charge card, leading to credit cards
51	•Minkowski finds 'rogue asteroid' Geographos	•Power steering for cars (Chrysler)	•Tindbergen's The Study of Instinct, animal behaviour	•Pedestrian or 'zebra' road crossings (UK)
52	•First nuclear accident at Chalk River, Canada	•Computer predictions for US Presidential election	•James van Allen devises a 'rockoon' balloon/rocket	•Transistor hearing aid •Part-transistor radio
53	•Watson and Crick discover DNA structure	•First use of a heart-lung machine for surgery	•Frederick Sanger works out structure of insulin hormone	•First concert on an electronic synthesizer
54	•Oral contraceptive pill begins limited tests	•Nuclear power makes electricity, Obninsk, USSR	•Linus Pauling receives Nobel Prize for chemistry	•Photovoltaic or 'solar' cells, electricity from light
55	•Massive radio telescope dish, Jodrell Bank, UK	•Optical fibres and hovercraft in development	•Albert Einstein dies	•Artificial diamonds
56	•First heart pacemakers undergo tests	•Magnetic videotape to record and edit TV shows	•John Backus' FORTRAN computer language (IBM)	•Battery-powered electric wristwatch
57	•USSR launches first satellite, Sputnik 1	•Fibre-optic endoscope to look into the body	•Hutchinson coins the term 'niche' in ecological science	•Radar 'traps' to catch speeding motorists (UK)
58	•Worldwide anti-nuclear campaigns begin	•Ultrasound scans to check unborn babies	•Van Allen's radiation layers around Earth	•Bifocal contact lenses •Computer chess program
59	•Dark side of the Moon photographed (USSR)	•First integrated circuits or microchips	•Grace Hopper's COBOL computer language	•Mass-market photocopier •Stereo LP vinyl discs

31

INDEX